BRITISH RAILWAYS STEAMING THROUGH THE SIXTIES

Volume Three

Compiled by
PETER HANDS & COLIN RICHARDS

DEFIANT PUBLICATIONS
190 Yoxall Road, Shirley,
Solihull, West Midlands.

Printed in the United Kingdom by Netherwood Dalton & Co Ltd, Huddersfield, England

ACKNOWLEDGEMENTS

Grateful thanks are extended to the following contributors of photographs not only for their use in this book but for their kind patience and long term loan of negatives/photographs whilst this book was being compiled.

G. D. APPLEYARD MIDDLESBROUGH.	P. BARBER TAMWORTH.	B. BUBB BIRMINGHAM.
P. CANE HATFIELD.	C. FIFIELD LONDON.	J. D. GOMERSALL SHEFFIELD.
R. GRACE BASINGSTOKE.	D. HARRISON CHAPELTOWN.	G. HARVEY WOODHAM FERRERS.
R. HENNEFER SUTTON COLDFIELD.	C. HUGHES AMESBURY.	A. C. INGRAM WISBECH.
D. K. JONES MOUNTAIN ASH.	H. N. JAMES IPSWICH	B. J. MILLER BARRY.
D. OAKES HITCHIN.	MRS. D. OAKES HITCHIN.	D. PETTITT ILMINSTER.
R. PICTON WOLVERHAMPTON.	W. G. PIGGOTT HADDENHAM.	B. RANDS WESTON-SUPER-MARE.
K. L. SEAL ANDOVERSFORD.	G. W. SHARPE BARNSLEY.	C. STACEY STONEY STRATFORD.
D. TITHERIDGE FAREHAM.	S. TURNBULL MILTON OF CAMPSIE.	R. TURNER SHEFFIELD.
A. WAKEFIELD DRONFIELD.	T. WALTON ISLEWORTH.	T. WARD NORTHAMPTON.
N. WELLINGS BEBINGTON.	B. WILSON SOLIHULL.	G. H. WILSON BIRMINGHAM.

Further books in this series which are available are as follows:

BRITISH RAILWAYS STEAMING THROUGH THE SIXTIES - Volume One.

BRITISH RAILWAYS STEAMING THROUGH THE SIXTIES - Volume Two.

BRITISH RAILWAYS STEAMING ON THE WESTERN REGION - Volume One.

Other titles available from DEFIANT PUBLICATIONS.

WHAT HAPPENED TO STEAM - Volumes 1 to 50.

CHASING STEAM ON SHED.

Front cover – SR Unrebuilt *Battle of Britain* Class 4-6-2 No 34086 *219 Squadron* waits to depart from London (Victoria) with the down *Golden Arrow* on 8th May 1960. (D. K. Jones)

INTRODUCTION

BRITISH RAILWAYS STEAMING THROUGH THE SIXTIES, Volume Three is the third of a series of books designed to give the ordinary, everyday steam photographic enthusiast of the 1960's a chance to participate in and give pleasure to others whilst recapturing the twilight days of steam.

In this series, wherever possible, no famous names will be found, but the content and quality of the majority of photographs will be second to none. The photographs chosen have been carefully selected to give a mixture of action and shed scenes from many parts of British Railways, whilst utilising a balanced cross-section of locomotives of GWR, SR, LMS, LNER & BR origins.

As steam declined, especially from 1966 onwards, the choice of locomotive classes and locations also dwindled. Rather than include the nowadays more traditional preserved locomotive photographs in the latter days of steam, the reader will find more locomotives of SR, LMS & BR backgrounds included towards the end of the book.

In an effort to reduce repetition of classes, the chapter on 1968 has been reduced slightly and a new chapter introduced to include scrapyards.

The majority of the photographs used in Volume Three have been contributed by readers of Peter Hands series of booklets entitled "What Happened to Steam" and from readers of Volumes One & Two of "BR Steaming Through the Sixties". In normal circumstances these may have been hidden from the public eye for ever.

The continuation of this series depends upon you the reader. If you feel you have suitable photographic material of B.R. steam locomotives from 1950-1968 and wish to contribute them towards this series and other future publications please contact either:

Peter Hands,   Colin Richards,
190 Yoxall Road,   28 Kendrick Close,
Shirley, Solihull,   OR   Damson Parkway, Solihull,
West Midlands B90 3RN.   West Midlands B92 0QD.

CONTENTS

NAMEPLATES – Nameplate examples of the five main representatives of British Railways.

1) GWR *Grange* Class 4-6-0 No 6860 *Aberporth Grange*. (D. K. Jones)

2) SR rebuilt *Merchant Navy* Class 4-6-2 No 35001 *Channel Packet*. (C. Stacey)

3) LMS *Jubilee* Class 4-6-0 No 45626 *Seychelles*. (R. Picton)

4) LNER B1 Class 4-6-0 No 61016 *Inyala*. (R. Picton)

5) BR *Clan* Class 4-6-2 No 72001 *Clan Cameron*. (R. Picton)

6) The front end details are clearly shown on this close-up picture of BR *Britannia* Class 4-6-2 No 70000 *Britannia* in the yard at 36A Doncaster in March 1960. *Britannia* is preserved on the Nene Valley Railway. (B. Wilson)

7)	LMS rebuilt *Patriot* Class 4-6-0 No 45523 *Bangor* is a visitor to 6G Llandudno Junction from 1B Camden shed on 22nd July 1960. (R. Picton)

8)	GWR *Grange* Class 4-6-0 No 6852 *Headbourne Grange* passes Ashley Hill on the outskirts of Bristol with a fitted freight on 21st June 1960. (R. Picton)

9) BR Class 3 2-6-2T No 82011 waits to leave Sidmouth Junction with the 9.28 am to Sidmouth on 14th April 1960. A number of these BR locomotives along with sister Class 4 2-6-4T's were allocated to 72A Exmouth Junction for local services on the south coast around Exeter. (R. Picton)

10) A4 Class 4-6-2 No 60007 *Sir Nigel Gresley* from 34A Kings Cross blows off steam in the shed yard at 34E New England on 21st August 1960. *Sir Nigel Gresley* is preserved in active service and is based at Steamtown, Carnforth. (R. Picton)

11) GWR 2800 Class 2-8-0 No 3836 and GWR *Castle* Class 4-6-0 No 5002 *Ludlow Castle* are both sporting fresh paint after overhaul at Swindon Works – June 1960. Although carrying an 85A Worcester shed-plate *Ludlow Castle* was not in fact allocated there and remained at 82C Swindon until November 1963. (R. Picton)

12) SR Class T9 (Greyhound) 4-4-0 No 30707 is photographed light engine near Eastleigh on 7th September 1960. All of the surviving members of this class with the exception of the preserved 30120 were all withdrawn by the end of 1961. (R. Picton)

13) LMS *Jubilee* Class 4-6-0 No 45576 *Bombay* in filthy external condition makes its way to 82E Bristol Barrow Road shed after bringing in the 12.48 pm express from York. Photographed at Bristol (Temple Meads) on 1st August 1960. (R. Picton)

14) LNER V2 Class 2-6-2 No 60814 speeds past Helpston Crossing with an express on 20th August 1960. (R. Picton)

15) 82A Bristol (Bath Road) was one of the few Western Region depots where a number of the GWR *County* Class 4-6-0's could be found at any one time. Photographed together in the shed yard are Nos 1011 *County of Chester* and 1014 *County of Glamorgan* on 19th June 1960 less than three months before Bath Road closed to steam. (R. Picton)

16) BR Class 2 2-6-0 No 78000 poses for the camera in the shed yard at 89C Machynlleth on 18th July 1960. Although officially closed in December 1966 diesel multiple units are still stabled on the site and part of the shed building is still intact. (R. Picton)

17) SR Class A1X 0-6-0 Tank No 32636 is seen in the shed yard at 71A Eastleigh on 5th March 1960. Their main source of employment when based at Eastleigh was on the Hayling Island branch. Eight members of this class are preserved including 32636 which can be found on the Bluebell Railway. (R. Picton)

18) BR Class 9F 2-10-0 No 92220 *Evening Star* still carrying express passenger headcode, drifts through Bristol (Temple Meads) light engine after bringing in the 2.45 pm passenger train from Portsmouth on 1st August 1960. *Evening Star* is part of the National Railway Museum collection and is used in active service. (R. Picton)

19) GWR *Modified Hall* Class 4-6-0 No 7924 *Thornycroft Hall* arrives at Bedminster in the Bristol suburbs with the 5.18 pm evening local to Taunton on 28th May 1960. (R. Picton)

20) LNER Class 04/1 2-8-0 No 63799 from 36C Frodingham is a visitor to 34E New England on 21st August 1960. Although introduces as early as 1911 some examples of the class survived in service until April 1966. (R. Picton)

21) LMS *Royal Scot* Class 4-6-0 No 46155 *The Lancer* speeds through Lichfield (Trent Valley) with an excursion on 15th July 1960. (G. H. Wilson)

22) LNER A4 Class 4-6-2 No 60015 *Quicksilver* leans to a curve through Peterborough with an east coast main line express on 20th August 1960. The first two coaches are of Gresley stock. (R. Picton)

23) SR M7 Class 0-4-4T No 30031 on station pilot duties at Waterloo on 4th September 1960. Waterloo was the last major London terminus to see regular steam services which survived until July 1967. (R. Picton)

24) BR Class 4 4-6-0 No 75012 from 6G Llandudno Junction is in ex. works condition in the shed yard at 17A Derby on 15th May 1960. The old lion and wheel emblem is still carried on the tender. (R. Picton)

25) SR Unrebuilt *West Country* Class 4-6-2 No 34006 *Bude* from 70A Nine Elms resides in the shed yard at 71A Eastleigh on 13th August 1961. (R. Picton)

26) LMS *Jubilee* Class 4-6-0 No 45668 *Madden* from 17A Derby rests in the shed yard at 82E Bristol Barrow Road on 28th August 1961. Members of this class were regular performers on the Bristol – Derby – Sheffield route until 1964/65. (D. K. Jones)

27) WD Class 2-8-0 No 90344 trundles through Stockton-on-Tees with a southbound mineral train in October 1961. This class earned itself the popular nickname of *Bed-Irons* due to their clanking motion. (G. D. Appleyard)

28) 9400 Class 0-6-0PT No 9400 at Swindon Works on 30th July 1961. Introduced during 1947 for heavy freight shunting 9400 was withdrawn in December 1959 after only twelve years service. Stored at Swindon for well over two years 9400 was restored and is now preserved at the Great Western Museum – Swindon. (R. Picton)

29) L & Y 0-4-0ST No 51218 at rest in front of the huge gasholder which was a prominent landmark by 82E Bristol Barrow Road on 9th July 1961. Withdrawn in September 1964 51218 is preserved on the Keighley & Worth Valley Railway. (R. Picton)

30) LNER Class A1 4-6-2 No 60138 *Boswell* drifts into Stockton-on-Tees station with the 1.00 pm express to Colchester on 12th November 1961. The crew of *Boswell* are taking full advantage of the protective tarpaulin between the roof of the cab and the tender. (G. D. Appleyard)

31) BR Class 2 2-6-2T No 84020 in use as a station pilot waits to remove empty stock at Exeter (Central) on 19th July 1961. In the background is SR N Class 2-6-0 No 31838. (R. Picton)

32) *Castle* Class 4-6-0 No 5061 *Earl of Birkenhead* departs from Mangotsfield with the Cornishman on 21st April 1961. (D. K. Jones)

33) BR Class 3 2-6-2T No 82024 in the shed yard at 72A Exmouth Junction on 19th July 1961. (R. Picton)

34) SR rebuilt *West Country* Class 4-6-2 No 34096 *Trevone* lifts its safety valves whilst waiting to depart from Exeter (St. Davids) with the 4.19 pm to Plymouth on 29th September 1961. (R. Picton)

35) LNER Class A1 4-6-2 No 60140 *Balmoral* reflects the rays of weak sunshine at 50A York shed in March 1961. (G. W. Sharpe)

36) BR Class 5 4-6-0 No 73170 from 55A Leeds (Holbeck) is photographed alongside the shed building at 82E Bristol (Barrow Road) in May 1961. Also present are a number of LMS types – 4F 0-6-0's and a *Crab* 2-6-0. (G. W. Sharpe)

37) GWR *Hall* Class 4-6-0 No 6935 *Browsholme Hall* in filthy external condition passes through Swindon with a down train of vans on 30th September 1961. (J. D. Gomersall)

38) SR B4 Class 0-4-0T No 30102 poses for the camera in the yard at 71A Eastleigh on 18th September 1961. Withdrawn in September 1963 30102 is now preserved at the Bressingham Steam Museum. Also present in this picture are SR G16 Class 4-8-0T No 30494 & BR Class 4 4-6-0 No 75066. (R. Picton)

39) LMS *Royal Scot* Class 4-6-0 No 46125 *3rd Carabinier* at Birmingham (New Street) during 1961 with a Wolverhampton (High Level) to Euston express. (G. W. Sharpe)

40) SR E1 Class 4-4-0 No 31019 (piloted by SR T9 Class 4-4-0 No 30117) is captured by the camera at Ashford with an Ian Allan special on 5th April 1961. (Christopher Fifield)

41) LMS Unrebuilt *Patriot* Class 4-6-0 No 45537 *Private E. Sykes V.C.* passes 2B Nuneaton shed, light engine, in May 1961. The last of these unrebuilt engines was withdrawn by November 1962 and the last surviving rebuilt example went in December 1965. (C. Hughes)

42) LNER A2 Class 4-6-2 No 60531 *Bahram* from 61B Aberdeen (Ferryhill) in steam in the shed yard at 64B Haymarket in October 1961. The *top link* Haymarket depot closed to steam in September 1963 and a diesel depot was built on the site. (G. W. Sharpe)

43) A busy scene in the yard at 82B St. Philips Marsh on 9th July 1961. On view is GWR 4200 Class 2-8-0T No 5224 (86E Severn Tunnel Jct.), an unidentified GWR *Castle* Class 4-6-0, GWR 1361 0-6-0ST No 1365 (82C Swindon) & GWR *Hall* Class 4-6-0 No 5901 *Hazel Hall* (81D Reading). (R. Picton)

44) LNER A2/3 Class 4-6-2 No 60500 *Edward Thompson* waits to leave Ferme Park goods yard (London) with an express freight to New England (Peterborough) on a wintry day in February 1962. (P. Cane)

45) BR *Britannia* Class 4-6-2 No 70030 *William Wordsworth* at York with a lengthy cross country express to Colchester on 4th May 1962. (D. K. Jones)

46) SR Rebuilt *West Country* Class 4-6-2 No 34027 *Taw Valley* and SR S15 Class 4-6-0 No 30499 are bathed in late afternoon sunlight at 71A Eastleigh on 11th February 1962. *Taw Valley* is now preserved on the North Yorkshire Moors Railway and 30499 is preserved on the Mid-Hants Railway. (R. Picton)

47) A quartet of GWR *Castle* Class 4-6-0's grace the shed yard at 87A Neath on 23rd April 1962. Nos 5051 *Earl Bathurst*, 4090 *Dorchester Castle*, 5062 *Earl of Shaftesbury* and 5078 *Beaufort* are all in good external condition. *Earl Bathurst* is preserved at G.W.S. Didcot. (R. Picton)

48) BR Class 9F 2-10-0 No 92120 from Leicester (Midland) is a visitor to 6F Bidston on 20th May 1962. This small dockland shed closed in February 1963. (D. Harrison)

49) GWR *Hall* Class 4-6-0 No 4916 *Crumlin Hall* (light engine) looks on as LMS *Royal Scot* Class 4-6-0 No 46125 *3rd Carabinier* arrives with the 1.10 pm express to Plymouth on 4th August 1962. Hereford still sees regular steam workings on specials and also is the location of the Bulmers Steam Centre. (R. Picton)

50) SR E4 Class 0-6-2T No 32503 is partially hidden by shrubbery whilst shunting freight wagons at Newhaven Town on 7th October 1962. (R. Picton)

51) GWR *Castle* Class 4-6-0 No 5075 *Wellington* about to leave the shed yard at 88A Cardiff (Canton) to work a special on 3rd June 1962. Canton closed to steam three months later most of its stock being transferred to Cardiff East Dock shed. (R. Picton)

52) LNER B1 Class 4-6-0 No 61375 overshadowed by electrification apparatus passes through Stratford station with empty coaching stock on 7th April 1962. (P. Cane)

53) LMS Class 4 2-6-4T No 42419 commences the descent of the Lickey Incline at Blackwell with the 5.40 pm Birmingham (New Street) – Worcester local passenger train on 25th August 1962. (R. Picton)

54) BR Class 5 4-6-0 No 73021 in immaculate condition poses outside 82F Bath Green Park on 15th August 1962. This shed came under W.R. control in February 1958 from the S.R. and finally closed in March 1966 along with most of the former S & D lines. (B. Bubb)

55) LMS *Royal Scot* Class 4-6-0 No 46115 *Scots Guardsman* is a visitor to 1A Willesden on 9th September 1962 from 9A Longsight (Manchester). *Scots Guardsman* was the last of the class to be withdrawn, in December 1965 and is preserved at Dinting. (R. Picton)

56) LNER D34 Class 4-4-0 No 62484 *Glen Lyon* in store at the notorious Bathgate dump on 5th August 1962. Withdrawn in November 1961 *Glen Lyon* was stored at Hawick and Bathgate for over 1½ years before being scrapped. (D. Harrison)

57) GWR *Modified Hall* Class 4-6-0 No 7929 *Wyke Hall* in use as a station pilot at Birmingham (Snow Hill) awaits its next turn of duty on 5th August 1962. (R. Picton)

58) BR Class 4 2-6-0 No 76054 passes light engine through Southampton Central in May 1962. (G. W. Sharpe)

59) LMS Class 2 2-6-0 No 46525 heads a line of GWR locomotives – 6100 Class 2-6-2T No 6147, 5700 Class 0-6-0PT No 3765 and *Hall* Class 4-6-0 No 5940 *Whitbourne Hall* in the shed yard at 82B St. Philips Marsh on 28th July 1962. All of these engines were based at this depot. (R. Picton)

60) GWR 5700 Class 0-6-0PT No 4669 from 88H Tondu heads a local passenger train at Bridgend on 23rd April 1962. (R. Picton)

61) LNER A3 Class 4-6-2 No 60062 *Minoru* at Doncaster Works after being outshopped in September 1962. This was the final form of the A3's – *Minoru's* double chimney was fitted in February 1959 and the German smoke deflectors in July 1961. (G. W. Sharpe)

62) SR 02 Class 0-4-4T No 16 *Ventnor* after arrival at its namesake station on the Isle of Wight with the 3.32 pm from Ryde on 14th July 1962. (R. Picton)

63) SR *Schools* Class 4-4-0 No 30928 *Stowe* – a fine close-up study of this locomotive prior to restoration. Taken at 75D Stewarts Lane in May 1963. *Stowe* is currently operating on the Bluebell Railway. (P. Cane)

64) LNER Class A4 4-6-2 No 60022 *Mallard* at Doncaster Works on 9th June 1963. This world speed record holder had been withdrawn in April 1963 and was externally restored by late 1963. *Mallard* is preserved in York Railway Museum. (G. W. Sharpe)

65) LMS Class 8F 2-8-0 No 48311 moves slowly through Rotherham Masborough on 21st October 1963 with a mineral train. (R. Picton)

66) BR *Britannia* Class 4-6-2 No 70051 *Firth of Forth* speeds through Roade Cutting with an up excursion to Euston on 25th May 1963. Nos 70050-54 were originally based at 66A Polmadie (Glasgow) but by October 1962 all were based at English depots. (Terry Ward)

67) GWR 6400 Class 0-6-0PT No 6435 at Tondu with a local passenger train on 8th June 1963. The local shed at Tondu a single roundhouse was located to the right of the picture. (D. K. Jones)

68) LNER B1 Class 4-6-0 No 61097 from 34E New England is an unusual visitor to 2E Northampton shed on 9th July 1963. (Terry Ward)

69) LMS Class 4 2-6-0 No 43106 complete with tablet catching apparatus is seen in the shed yard at 1A Willesden on 27th March 1963. At this time 43106 was based at 15B Kettering. Withdrawn from Lostock Hall shed in June 1968, 43106 now resides on the Severn Valley Railway. (D. K. Jones)

70) LMS *Royal Scot* Class 4-6-0 No 46168 *The Girl Guide* pilots B.R. *Britannia* Class 4-6-2 No 70034 *Thomas Hardy* on a heavy northbound express freight near Northampton (Kingsthorpe) on 16th September 1963. (Terry Ward)

71) GWR *Grange* Class 4-6-0 No 6856 *Stowe Grange* from 85A Worcester simmers gently by the coal stage at 82B St. Philips Marsh on 28th July 1963. (R. Picton)

72) BR Class 4 4-6-0 No 75068 from 71A Eastleigh is in ex. works condition in the shed yard at Fratton on 7th April 1963. Fratton had its own code (70F) until November 1959 when it became a sub shed. (B. Rands)

73) SR W Class 2-6-4T No 31924 blows off steam after assisting a train into Exeter Central up the 1 in 37 bank from Exeter (St. Davids) on 3rd August 1963. (R. Picton)

74) BR *Britannia* Class 4-6-2 No 70050 *Firth of Clyde* (5A Crewe North) stands in mint condition along with BR Class 3 2-6-2T No 82038 (82E Bristol Barrow Road) after overhaul at Crewe Works on 15th September 1963. (B. Rands)

75) Ex. Caledonian Railway Class 3P 4-4-0 No 54482 and LMS Class 3 2-6-2T No 40150 are both condemned and in store at 63A Perth on 13th April 1963. (B. Rands)

76) SR Rebuilt *Merchant Navy* Class 4-6-2 No 35001 *Channel Packet* accelerates an up express out of Weymouth on 1st June 1963. (B. Wilson)

77) GWR *King* Class 4-6-0 No 6018 *King Henry VI* departs from Southall with an S.L.S. special from Birmingham (Snow Hill) – Swindon on 28th April 1963. Although withdrawn in December 1962 *King Henry VI* had been retained at 84E Tyseley for use on this special. (P. Cane)

78) LNER A4 Class 4-6-2 No 60025 *Falcon* arrives at Hitchin with a down express from Kings Cross on 12th May 1963 a few short weeks away from regular steam services between Kings Cross and Peterborough ceasing. (D. Oakes)

79) SR 700 Class 0-6-0 No 30368 and SR *Schools* Class 4-4-0 No 30934 *St. Lawrence* lie condemned and unwanted in Basingstoke goods yard in late February 1963 prior to removal to Eastleigh Works for scrapping. (R. Grace)

80) 81C Southall shed on 21st April 1963. Peeping out of the shed building are GWR locomotives – 2800 Class 2-8-0 No 2899, *Modified Hall* Class 4-6-0 No 7923 *Speke Hall*, 2800 Class 2-8-0 No 3819 (81E Didcot) and 9400 Class 0-6-0PT No 8426. (H. N. James)

81) BR Class 5 4-6-0 No 73080 *Merlin* leaves Bath Spa with the 1.30 pm relief express to Weymouth on 10th August 1963. (R. Picton)

82) LNER Q6 Class 0-8-0's Nos 63458 from 52F Blyth and 63367 at rest outside the straight shed 52G Sunderland on 9th May 1964. Sunderland shed remained open to steam until September 1967. (R. Hennefer)

83) SR Unrebuilt *Battle of Britain* Class 4-6-2 No 34066 *Spitfire* passes Basingstoke shed with the 11.16 am Bournemouth – Waterloo express on 13th September 1964. (D. K. Jones)

84) BR Class 9F 2-10-0 No 92213 is in filthy condition in the yard at 2D Banbury on 7th June 1964. Many examples of this fine class had short working lives, in the case of 92213 just seven years. (Terry Ward)

85) GWR *Manor* Class 4-6-0 No 7820 *Dinmore Manor* at Craven Arms & Stokesay station with a short freight on 25th April 1964. *Dinmore Manor* was to be restored at the Gwili Railway but has now been moved to the West Somerset Railway. (R. Picton)

86) LMS Class 2 2-6-0 No 46521 arrives at Towyn with the 3.58 pm local to Machynlleth on 17th July 1964. Towyn was and still is the location of the Talyllyn Railway, a superb narrow gauge railway. (R. Picton)

87) LNER Class Y9 0-4-0ST No 68095 outside 64F Bathgate shed on 30th March 1964. Some of these diminutive locomotives were fitted with wooden tenders, somewhat of a fire risk one would have thought. 68095 is preserved at Lytham Museum. (N. Wellings)

88) Reading South shed on the Southern Region was situated parallel to the Western Region main line. On 29th August 1964 SR U Class 2-6-0 No 31791 from 70C Guildford was in steam in the shed yard. (C. Stacey)

89) GWR 7200 Class 2-8-2T No 7221 simmers in the weed covered yard at 2D Banbury on 31st May 1964. (Terry Ward)

90) BR Class 9F 2-10-0 No 92080 on the Midland main line at Hathern, north of Loughborough with a southbound Class 8 ballast train on 11th April 1964. (K. L. Seal)

91) SR Unrebuilt *Battle of Britain* Class 4-6-2 No 34063 *229 Squadron* at speed west of Basingstoke with the 1.00 pm Waterloo – Exeter express on 3rd April 1964. (R. Grace)

92) LMS *Jubilee* Class 4-6-0 No 45666 *Cornwallis* from 8B Warrington is in the shed yard at 1A Willesden on 19th April 1964. (D. K. Jones)

93) LMS Class 8F 2-8-0 No 48309 from 87F Llanelly is in steam outside the small sub shed at Craven Arms on 25th April 1964. (R. Picton)

94) LNER Class J38 0-6-0 No 65934 from 62C Dunfermline is in steam at Alloa sub shed on 27th March 1964. All of this class of thirty-five engines were based in Scotland and some members survived until April 1967. (B. Rands)

95) BR ex. Crosti-boilered Class 9F 2-10-0 No 92027 darkens the Midland main line north of Loughborough, with a southbound Class 8 mixed freight train on 11th April 1964. (K. L. Seal)

96) GWR 2800 Class 2-8-0 No 2898 travels light engine near Banbury on 11th April 1964. (D. K. Jones)

97) GWR *Hall* Class 4-6-0 No 5971 *Merevale Hall* from Old Oak Common shed poses in front of the coal stage at 82B St. Philips Marsh on 8th March 1964, three months before closure. (R. Picton)

98) LMS Class 5 4-6-0 No 45220 at Bamford with a Chinley to Sheffield local passenger train in June 1964. The leading coach is of Gresley vintage. (D. Pettitt)

99) LNER A4 Class 4-6-2 No 60006 *Sir Ralph Wedgwood* is about to depart from Perth with an Aberdeen – Glasgow
(Buchanan Street) express in 1964. Through trains to Aberdeen now use the platforms on the right of the picture and
go via Dundee instead of Forfar. (G. W. Sharpe)

100) SR 02 Class 0-4-4T's Nos 20 *Shanklin* and 29 *Alverstone* outside 70H Ryde shed on 20th September 1964.
(R. Picton)

101) Steam leaking from various places, a home-made numberplate, no shedplate, grimy and stripped of nameplates – the decline of steam is epitomized in this photograph of 86E Severn Tunnel Junction GWR *Hall* Class 4-6-0 No 6944 *Fledborough Hall* at 82E Bristol Barrow Road on 14th November 1965, one week before closure. (R. Picton)

102) BR Class 9F 2-10-0 No 92239 from 50A York is surrounded by ex. LMS types at 2D Banbury shed on 5th June 1965. (C. Stacey)

103) SR Rebuilt *Merchant Navy* Class 4-6-2 No 35014 *Nederland Line* at 75B Redhill on 14th March 1965. *Nederland Line* from 70G Weymouth had failed with a hot box on a railtour special. (C. Stacey)

104) LMS Class 4 2-6-0 No 43044 is in company with two unidentified LMS Class 8F 2-8-0's at 55B Stourton on 29th August 1965. The LMS Class 4 2-6-0's were often referred to as *Flying Pigs*. (R. Picton)

105) BR Class 4 2-6-4T No 80065 in steam in the shed yard at 70D Eastleigh on 6th November 1965. (D. Titheridge)

106) GWR 5700 Class 0-6-0PT No 3767 awaits the next call to duty acting as a station pilot at Newport (High Street) on 19th April 1965. (R. Picton)

107) LNER A4 Class 4-6-2 No 60009 *Union of South Africa* waits at Stonehaven before restarting the up *Grampion* express to Glasgow (Buchanan Street) on 8th June 1965. The fine sight of *Union of South Africa* can still be seen as this locomotive is preserved in active service in Scotland. (K. L. Seal)

108) SR Rebuilt *Battle of Britain* Class 4-6-2 No 34071 *601 Squadron* completes a fine picture of Bournemouth Central on 26th June 1965. *601 Squadron* is on the 1.30 pm Weymouth to Waterloo express. (R. Picton)

109) Ex. North British Class J37 0-6-0 No 64577 stands at Montrose, sub-shed to 62B Dundee Tay Bridge on 9th June 1965. (K. L. Seal)

110) GWR 5700 Class 0-6-0PT No 7760 in the guise of London Transport No L90 at 70D Eastleigh after overhaul at Eastleigh Works on 6th December 1965. 7760 had been withdrawn from B.R. service in January 1962 and survived until June 1971 with the L.T.R. Now preserved at Birmingham Railway Museum. (D. Titheridge)

111) LMS Class 5 4-6-0 No 44879 reverses into Coupar Angus station prior to departing with the 4.07 pm mail train from Aberdeen on 9th June 1965. (K. L. Seal)

112) SR Q1 Class 0-6-0 No 33026 light engine at Guildford on 17th July 1965. Aesthetically speaking these locomotives must rank as amongst the ugliest on British Railways. (W. G. Piggott)

113) Ex. North British Class J37 0-6-0 No 64599 drifts into Dunfermline with a trip freight working on 27th August 1965. (C. Richards)

114) GWR *Grange* Class 4-6-0 No 6859 *Yiewsley Grange* is devoid of nameplates but in surprisingly good condition as it leaves Banbury shed on 13th November 1965 sporting an express headcode. Despite carrying an 86E Severn Tunnel Junction shedplate *Yiewsley Grange* had been transferred to 81F Oxford. (D. Titheridge)

115) BR Class 3 2-6-T No 82018 poses for the camera outside 70A Nine Elms on 7th March 1965. From late 1962 a number of these engines were drafted to Nine Elms mostly for use on carriage duties between Waterloo and Clapham Junction. (C. Stacey)

116) SR Rebuilt *West Country* 4-6-2 No 34100 *Appledore* in beautiful condition graces the shed yard at 70D Eastleigh on 6th December 1965. Based at 70E Salisbury, *Appledore* is a splendid example of how this shed looked after most of its engines right up to the end of steam on the Southern. (D. Titheridge)

117) BR Class 5 4-6-0 No 73083 *Pendragon* pauses at Southampton Central with an up freight on 29th September 1965. (J. D. Gomersall)

118) LNER 01 Class 2-8-0 No 63646 in the shed yard at 41H Staveley G.C. on 7th June 1965. This shed closed a week later, 63646 was subsequently transferred to 41J Langwith Jct. but withdrawn the following month. (C. Stacey)

119) LMS Class 5 4-6-0 No 45376 from 8A Edge Hill (Liverpool) in the unusual surroundings of Nottingham Victoria station at the head of the 08.15 am express to Marylebone on 3rd September 1965. The demise of this grand station is already apparent, some tracks have already been lifted and the state of the roof leaves something to be desired. (D. K. Jones)

120) Carrying a wreath a grimy LMS Class 5 4-6-0 No 44984 based at 16B Colwick stands at Woodford Halse station with one of the last services over the former G.C. main line on the final day of its existence – 3rd September 1966. (W. G. Piggott)

121) SR Rebuilt *Battle of Britain* Class 4-6-2 No 34089 *602 Squadron* stands at Brighton with the LCGB *Reunion Railtour* on 10th December 1966. (C. Richards)

122) BR *Britannia* Class 4-6-2 No 70022 *Tornado* from 12B Carlisle (Upperby) is a visitor to 5B Crewe (South) on 15th June 1966. The *Britannia's* used to carry handrails on the smoke deflectors but after an accident to 70026 *Polar Star* in 1955 these were removed to obtain better visibility. (D. K. Jones)

123) LMS Class 5 4-6-0 No 45493 based at 2D Banbury rolls into Basingstoke with the 10.30 am Poole – York express on 30th May 1966. Note that the third rails are in position for the forthcoming electrification. (J. D. Gomersall)

124) BR Class 4 2-6-4T No 80082 shunts at Brockenhurst on 18th August 1966. (A. C. Ingram)

125) SR Rebuilt *West Country* Class 4-6-2 No 34008 *Padstow* is photographed out of steam in the shed yard at 70A Nine Elms on 29th August 1966. (J. D. Gomersall)

126) LNER B1 Class 4-6-0 No 61035 from 50A York stands in the yard at 55E Normanton shed on 20th September 1966. 61035 was formerly named *Pronghorn*. (A. Wakefield)

127) LMS Class 5 4-6-0 No 45299 stands inside 2D Banbury shed on 25th May 1966. This former GWR shed had lost its last GW locomotives by October 1965 having been taken over by ex. LMS and BR types. (D. Oakes)

128) LNER A2 Class 4-6-2 No 60532 *Blue Peter* at Aberdeen in December 1966 with an up express. *Blue Peter* was withdrawn the same month and is now preserved at Dinting. (D. Titheridge)

129) LMS Class 5 4-6-0 No 44871 from 9B Stockport takes on water on a cold and wet 4th February 1966 at Basingstoke with a Bournemouth – York express. (W. G. Piggott)

130) WD Class 8F 2-8-0 No 90272 from 50B Hull (Dairycoates) blows steam from its cylinder cocks in the yard at 55D Royston on 20th September 1966. (R. Turner)

131) Ex. North British J37 Class 0-6-0's Nos 64570 and 64618 blow off steam at Alloa during a photo-stop with an enthusiasts special on 25th June 1966. (R. Hennefer)

132) SR Unrebuilt *West Country* Class 4-6-2 No 34094 *Mortehoe* near Farnborough with an express on 28th May 1966. (Mrs. D. Oakes)

133) GWR 5100 Class 2-6-2T No 4176, GWR 5700 Class 0-6-0PT No 3625 and LMS Class 2 2-6-0 No 46428 in run down condition at the partly demolished shed at 2A Tyseley on 26th June 1966. 4176 withdrawn in October 1965 was in use on and off as a stationary boiler until March 1967. No 46428 is at the Strathspey Railway. (T. Walton)

134) LNER B1 Class 4-6-0 No 61102 is shrouded in steam outside 62B Dundee Tay Bridge shed on 16th July 1966. Note the unusual number of rivets on the tender. (C. Stacey)

135) One of the shunters at Crewe Works LMS Class 3F 0-6-0T No 47615 is observed out of steam on 3rd April 1966. The use of steam shunters at Crewe Works ceased in October 1966. (P. Cane)

136) LMS Class 8F 2-8-0 No 48622 fitted with a small snowplough arrives at Skipton with a freight from the Leeds area on 23rd May 1966. (R. Picton)

137) Steam had mostly ceased on the W.R. at the end of 1965. BR Class 5 4-6-0 No 73065 from 70A Nine Elms intrudes on W.R. territory at Westbury on 13th November 1966 with an enthusiasts special. (C. Richards)

138) SR Unrebuilt *West Country* Class 4-6-2 No 34015 *Exmouth* from 70E Salisbury is in steam in the shed yard at 70C Guildford on 27th March 1966. (W. G. Piggott)

139) LMS Class 5 4-6-0 No 44821 at rest inside 5B Crewe (South) shed on 4th June 1967. Crewe (South) closed to steam in November 1967. (P. Barber)

140) LNER B1 Class 4-6-0 No 61072 in store at 62B Dundee Tay Bridge after withdrawal. Photographed on 10th July 1967 some two months after the closure of the shed. (S. Turnbull)

141) BR *Britannia* Class 4-6-2 No 70029 *Shooting Star* sweeps down from Shap and through Tebay station with a southbound afternoon parcels train on 22nd September 1967. On the right of the picture is the former line to Darlington which had been closed for a number of years. (W. G. Piggott)

142) A line-up of steam locomotives at 8F Springs Branch Wigan shed on 27th August 1967 includes LMS Class 8F 2-8-0 No 48474 (5B Crewe South), BR *Britannia* Class 4-6-2 No 70029 *Shooting Star* (12A Carlisle Kingmoor), BR Class 5 4-6-0 No 73011 (9H Patricroft) and LMS Class 5 4-6-0 No 44911 (12A Carlisle Kingmoor). (R. Picton)

143) SR Rebuilt *West Country* Class 4-6-2 No 34021 *Dartmoor* is in clean condition but minus nameplates at 70A Nine Elms on 30th April 1967. Nine Elms closed to steam in early July 1967. (R. Hennefer)

144) LMS Class 5 4-6-0 No 45089 blackens the countryside near Hale with an express on 20th June 1967. (D. K. Jones)

145) BR Class 4 2-6-4T No 80151 at Eastleigh, light engine, on 19th April 1967 is in good external condition despite being only one month away from withdrawal. (R. Picton)

146) LMS Class 5 4-6-0 No 44983 and BR *Britannia* Class 4-6-2 No 70023 *Venus* (12A Carlisle Kingmoor) stand amidst the dirt and grime of 55A Leeds (Holbeck) shed on 30th August 1967 a month or so before closure to steam. (S. Turnbull)

147) SR Rebuilt *West Country* Class 4-6-2 No 34093 *Saunton* (minus nameplates) is about to leave Southampton Central with a down engineers train on 1st May 1967. (G. Harvey)

148) LMS Class 5 4-6-0 No 44819 climbs to Ribblehead Viaduct with a northbound freight on 22nd September 1967. (W. G. Piggott)

149) LMS Class 5 4-6-0's Nos 45226 (10D Lostock Hall) & 45212 (12A Carlisle Kingmoor) along with LMS Class 8F 2-8-0 No 48522 (5B) blend in nicely with the grimy surroundings at 5B Crewe (South) on 27th August 1967. 45212 is preserved on the Keighley & Worth Valley Railway. (R. Picton)

150) BR *Britannia* Class 4-6-2 No 70013 *Oliver Cromwell* in immaculate condition but minus nameplates is photographed at Crewe with a fitted freight on 22nd July 1967. *Oliver Cromwell* is preserved at Bressingham Steam Museum. (C. Richards)

151) S.R. Rebuilt *Merchant Navy* Class 4-6-2 No 35028 *Clan Line*, in good condition but again minus nameplates climbs Upwey Bank near Wishing Well Halt with a Weymouth to Waterloo express on 13th July 1967, less than one month before the end of steam on the Southern. *Clan Line* is now owned by the M.N.L.P.S. (W. G. Piggott)

152) LMS Class 4 2-6-0 No 43088 and LMS Class 8F 2-8-0 No 48697 are both in steam in front of the entrance to the roundhouse at 6C Croes Newydd on 29th April 1967. This shed closed to steam a few weeks later. (D. K. Jones)

153) SR USA Class 0-6-0T No 30064 is in excellent condition on shed at 70D Eastleigh on 25th March 1967. This class was used almost exclusively around the docks at Southampton for many years. 30064 is preserved on the Bluebell Railway. (C. Richards)

154) BR Class 4 4-6-0 No 75037 is under the coaling plant at 12E Tebay on 22nd September 1967. Tebay shed closed to steam at the end of 1967 and has since been demolished. (W. G. Piggott)

155) LMS Class 5 4-6-0's Nos 44895 and 45454 both look in reasonable working condition in front of the shed building at 9E Trafford Park on 5th February 1967. Trafford Park continued to house steam locomotives into 1968. (A. Wakefield)

156) BR Class 9F 2-10-0 No 92203 enjoys the warm summer sunshine in the yard at 9F Heaton Mersey on 15th August 1967. Based at 8H Birkenhead from September 1966 until withdrawal in November 1967, 92203 was stored at 5B Crewe (South) and is now preserved on the East Somerset Railway. (A. Wakefield)

157) LMS Class 8F 2-8-0 No 48503 faces an unidentified sister engine in the yard at 9F Heaton mersey on the same day 15th August 1967. Like most of the Manchester sheds, Heaton Mersey survived into 1968. (A. Wakefield)

158) This fine study of LMS Class 8F 2-8-0 No 48730 by the coal stage at 10F Rose Grove on 18th July 1968 sums up what steam shed life was really all about especially towards the end of steam – thankless and dirty. (C. Stacey)

159) As BR *Britannia* Class 4-6-2 No 70013 *Oliver Cromwell* was the last Pacific to survive into 1968 in normal service it is not surprising that many photographs were taken of this particular locomotive. Seen at Manchester (Victoria) on 11th August 1968, the last day of steam on B.R. (A. C. Ingram)

160) Four LMS Class 8F 2-8-0's (none of which can be identified) stand condemned and unwanted inside the closed shed at 9F Heaton Mersey on 3rd June 1968. The shed had been closed the previous month. (C. Stacey)

161) Sunlight picks out a trio of LMS Class 5 4-6-0's Nos 45203, 45420 and 44803 in the yard of their home based shed at 9D Newton Heath on 14th April 1968. Newton Heath closed its doors to steam on 1st July 1968. (R. Picton)

162) Along with 8A Edge Hill, the shed at 8C Speke Junction survived into 1968 to represent steam in Liverpool. BR 9F 2-10-0 No 92162 is in store in the shed yard on 18th February 1968. Speke Junction closed around May 1968. (C. Richards)

163) 10A Carnforth was the last shed in the North-West to close to steam in August 1968 and has since become a major steam preservation centre. On 20th July 1968 LMS Class 5 4-6-0 No 45390 is amongst a line of out of steam sister engines. (C. Richards)

164) BR Class 5 4-6-0 No 73040 condemned and minus motion is in store outside 9H Patricroft on 1st June 1968. The shed itself closed exactly one month later. (G. Harvey)

165) LMS Class 5 4-6-0 No 44963 waits in Carnforth goods yard with a freight on 16th April 1968. (R. Picton)

166) A line of water columns overlook a trio of LMS tenders at 10D Lostock Hall shed on 20th April 1968. The left-hand tender belongs to LMS Class 5 4-6-0 No 44713. Lostock Hall closed in August 1968. (C. Richards)

167) A sparkling BR Class 4 4-6-0 No 75019 pilots an enthusiasts special at Carnforth in early August 1968. (A. C. Ingram)

168) LMS Class 5 4-6-0 No 44683 is seen after withdrawal in store at 10D Lostock Hall on 13th May 1968. (C. Richards)

169) LMS Class 5 4-6-0's Nos 44871 & 44781 approach Ais Gill on the Carlisle – Manchester section of the B.R. farewell to steam tour of 11th August 1968. No 44871 is preserved at Steamtown, Carnforth. (W. G. Piggott)

170) LMS Class 5 4-6-0 No 45156 takes refreshment at 10A Carnforth after arriving with a Society special on 4th August 1968. 45156 used to carry the name *Ayrshire Yeomanry* and on 4th August had a 65B St. Rollox shedplate, this being a Scottish shed that 45156 was once allocated to. (W. G. Piggott)

171) LMS Class 8F 2-8-0 No 48278 with painted number and shedcode, takes on coal at 10F Rose Grove in July 1968. (A. C. Ingram)

172) BR *Britannia* Class 4-6-2 No 70013 *Oliver Cromwell* in immaculate condition outside 10A Carnforth shed on 11th April 1968. (W. G. Piggott)

CHAPTER TEN - SCRAPYARDS

173) The remains of SR Z Class 0-8-0T No 30951 are just about recognisable after the cutters torch has been at work. Withdrawn from 72A Exmouth Junction in November 1962, 30951 had remained in store there until removal in January 1964, and photographed at Eastleigh Works in March 1964. (R. Grace)

174) At Thomas Ward's scrapyard, Beighton, Sheffield on 8th December 1965, LNER A1 Class 4-6-2 No 60154 *Bon Accord* is still intact, a start has been made on sister engine 60131 *Osprey* and LMS Class 8F 2-8-0 No 48401 is well on its way to destruction. (A. Wakefield)

175) BR Class 3 2-6-2T No 82035 stands forlornly in the yard at Cashmores, Newport, surrounded by piles of scrap that were once proud locomotives – 11th September 1965. (C. Stacey)

176) Three 4-6-0's, once the pride of the G.W.R. passenger engine stud, await the inevitable at Swindon Works scrapyard on 5th October 1963 – *Castle* Class No 4074 *Caldicot Castle*, *County* Class No 1023 *County of Oxford* and *Hall* Class No 5993 *Kirby Hall*. (B. J. Miller)

CHAPTER ELEVEN - PRESERVED LOCOMOTIVES

177) LMS Class 2 2-6-2T No 41312 had been reserved at Barry Docks since November 1972. Photographed in April 1974, 41312 was removed from Barry in August 1974 and is preserved by the Caerphilly Railway Society. (C. Richards)

178) GWR 5100 Class 2-6-2T No 4150 awaits removal to the Severn Valley Railway in April 1974, from Barry Docks. (C. Richards)

179) BR Class 8P 4-6-2 No 71000 *Duke of Gloucester*, partially restored externally, at Barry in April 1974. The *Duke* has been at Loughborough ever since and has had to undergo extensive rebuilding over many years. (C. Richards)